Able Was I
Ere
I Saw Elba

By the same author

Poetry
An Armada of Thirty Whales
A Little Geste
The City of Satisfactions
Striking the Stones
Broken Laws
The Center of Attention

Criticism
Poe Poe Poe Poe Poe Poe Poe
Barbarous Knowledge
Form and Fable in American Fiction
American Poetry and Poetics
The Poetry of Stephen Crane
Paul Bunyan, Last of the Frontier Demigods

For Peter Stitt –
Come to Philadelphia again!

Able Was I
Ere
I Saw Elba

Selected Poems 1954-74

~~Daniel Hoffman~~

Daniel Hoffman (signature)

Hutchinson of London

For Liz

Hutchinson & Co (Publishers) Ltd
3 Fitzroy Square, London W1

London Melbourne Sydney Auckland
Wellington Johannesburg and agencies
throughout the world

First published 1977
© in this collection Daniel Hoffman 1977

Set in Monotype Bembo

Printed in Great Britain by The Anchor Press Ltd
and bound by Wm Brendon & Son Ltd
both of Tiptree, Essex

ISBN 0 09 128241 1

Contents

From 'The Center of Attention' (1974)

Able Was I
Ere
I Saw Elba

From 'An Armada of Thirty Whales'

Incubus

What did the caterpillars do
last time the Phoenix died?
  They beat their breasts with a hundred fists
till one of them espied
the egg the ashes incubate.
Then, sure that wings would flame again,
they broke their bread on a mulberry leaf
and out of himself each wove the sheath
from which he'll burst on flaming wings
    after the peace of a season's sleep,
    after the peace of a season's sleep.

What did the little children do
when Christ was last time crucified?
  Each hid beneath a mulberry wreath
and on one another spied.
For they were playing Prisoner's Base
and as the teams hid face to face
the only thing that mattered much
was which was caught and which would catch
    before the evening grew more dark,
    before the earth and air grew dark.

The seals in Penobscot Bay

hadn't heard of the atom bomb,
so I shouted a warning to them.

Our destroyer (on trial run) slid by
the rocks where they gamboled and played;

they must have misunderstood,
or perhaps not one of them heard

me over the engines and tides.
As I watched them over our wake

I saw their sleek skins in the sun
ripple, light-flecked, on the rock,

plunge, bubbling, into the brine,
and couple & laugh in the troughs

between the waves' whitecaps and froth.
Then the males clambered clumsily up

and lustily crowed like seacocks,
sure that their prowess held thrall

all the sharks, other seals, and seagulls.
And daintily flipped the females,

seawenches with musical tails;
each looked at the Atlantic as

though it were her looking-glass.
If my warning had ever been heard

it was sound none would now ever heed.
And I, while I watched those far seals,

tasted honey that buzzed in my ears
and saw, out to windward, the sails

of an obsolete ship with banked oars
that swept like two combs through the spray

And I wished for a vacuum of wax
to ward away all those strange sounds,

yet I envied the sweet agony
of him who was tied to the mast,

when the boom, when the boom, when the boom
of guns punched dark holes in the sky.

An armada of thirty whales

(Galleons in sea-pomp) sails
over the emerald ocean.

The ceremonial motion
of their ponderous race is

given dandiacal graces
in the ballet of their geysers.

Eyes deep-set in whalebone vizors
have found a Floridian beach;

they leave their green world to fish.
Like the Pliocene midge, they declare

their element henceforth air.
What land they walk upon

becomes their Holy Land;
when these pilgrims have all found tongue

how their canticles shall be sung!
They nudge the beach with their noses,

eager for hedgerows and roses;
they raise their great snouts from the sea

and exulting gigantically
each trumpets a sousaphone wheeze

and stretches his finfitted knees.
But they who won't swim and can't stand

lie mired in mud and in sand,
And the sea and the wind and the worms

will contest the last will of the Sperms.

That the pear delights me now

That the pear's boughs
delight me now is
inconsequential.

But after fragrance come
bull bumblebees.
On ozone wings they hum,

on hairyhorny knees
rudely they enter,
nuzzle, gnash, & guzzle

nectar of the pear.
Roistering honeymakers,
wholly unaware

of the dust their bristles brought,
of the lovestrong draught
they pour down those pear-pistils.

It's June now, and the petals
have dropped, dried, crumbled,
in dust they've blown away.

Bees snarl in thick thistles;
pearboughs, hung in the hot day,
sprout green nubs now. Birdcalls

drench the leaves like fragrance;
fruit grows opulent in
summer lightning, heat, rains.

Sensuous the pears hang
richly, sweet and bursting.
Pears plop down. Birds follow, thirsting.

Nights nip the earthskin tighter,
sap stops of a morning,
sunred leaves more harshly flutter;

old pears the starling pecked at
wrinkle in the waning shade.
Fruit sourly lies, rejected

till it's out of the earth invaded:
maggots rapaciously & noiseless
fatten on fermented juices

and the gristle wriggles through
their sniggling tails & slime
spreads beneath the peartree.

Some squush remains, though,
some meat around the seed.
When Indian Summer strains

the last warmth through the orchard
pearpits feast and feed
and stir, & burst, & breed:

Earthward plunge the tendrils.
That the pear delighted me
is wholly incidental,

for the flower was for the fruit,
the fruit is for the seed.

The clams

In the Bay of Fundy the clams
lie stranded, half-dry, by the tides

forty feet higher than sea
in killdeer's kingdom.

Underground, they erect valved snouts.
Wet freckles sprout over the beach:

Each trickles a droplet, and each
attests to the desperate hope

that attends each ritual drop.
Lie ten-hours-buried in sand

and the swirl of salt and the wet
seems an Age before suffering began.

All shrinks in the rage of the sun
save the courage of clams, and their faith:

Sacrificing the water they breathe
seems to urge the tall moon from her orbit;

she tugs ocean, cubit by cubit
over killdeer's kingdom

and ends parched freedom.
Moon, with sky-arching shell

and bright snout nine thousand miles long
and anemones in her kelp hair

that gleam in the heaven around her,
responds with the wave of their prayers

or sucks the sea unawares.

Old Bug up there

On Faneuil Hall there squats a copper
more-than-man-sized green grasshopper.

Impaled above the Farmers' Market,
snow-slow smoke and sleet have darkened

him. His mandibles munch the seedless wind.
No hunger's his, no brass caresses;

he leaps the rooftops toward no granary.
Lashed by acerb winds he spins

to point the way. But men are heedless.
    Old Bug, you remind me of someone,

like you above a city raised
to seem far larger than alive.

You're not the only one that's placed
on such an eminence. And if

fewer follow your globe-eyed gaze now
than when this harbor was spined with masts,

I'll tell you bluntly, you're not first
nor last to point out true unfollowed ways.

The larks

An exaltation of larks arising
With elocutionary tongue
Embellish sound on morning air
Already fringed with scent of dung;
The curate in his curacy
Hearkens to that natural song,
And maids like wood-doves in their purity
Rise to matins' golden dong.
Their prayers are sweet high exultations
Whereon untrammeled spirits wend,
Forgetting flesh and breakfast. Under
The rectory eaves, the larks descend.

The voice of the woodthrush, played at half speed,

reveals to the halting ear
the fullstopt organ that pours through floodgate reed
such somersaults of sound like waters falling
in dark crystal chambers
on iron timbrels

withholds from what we hear
those haunting basses, loud but too deepkeyed.
This slow bisected bird's yet wilder calling
resounds on inward anvil:
pain is mortal, mortal.

Auricle's oracle

Intensity, when greatest, may
Prove ludicrously small.
Who concentrates compellingly
More than the snoutish snail,
Hauling gunless turret up
Perpendicular glass,
   By muscle of mind and bodily ooze advancing,
   Atop at last the aquarium glass balancing?

Yet passion at its most intense
Consumes the minuscule.
The focus of the spirit's lens
On whatever the self may will
Like sunlight squeezed through a reading-glass
Turns trash to flame. The ooze congeals
   In a golden signature of snail-identity,
   Etched in glass by the snail's and the sun's intensity.

Ephemeridæ

Dark specks whirr like lint alive in the sunlight.
The sky above the birches is disturbed.

Swarms swarm between pure heaven and treetops:
it's the mayflies' four-hour frenzy before their fall.

Waterward, they lay eggs in their dying
spasms, having then endured it all.

   For five long shimmering afternoons that summer
we walked beneath the birchgroves on the shore

and watched the empty light on leaftips pour
and out of nowhere whirled the nebulae,

gadding gilded, all green energy, toward death.
   After, the birches stirred, and we beneath

saw south-flying mallards bleak the air.
Green turns husk now. The world's shrunk to the bone.

   Our thin flesh alone
through this long, cold, fruitless season

scampers frantic in wild whirligig motion
while larvae of the mayfly wait

and mallards migrate and the sap runs slow;
ours alone from time strains to purchase

   pleasures mayflies find among the birches.

I dreamt my love a-dying lay

while I beside her stood austere
to see my paradise decay;
From underneath the ground I heard
her tunnelled agony of despair
ricochet from earth to air;
I learned the word that Adam's ear
in Eden heard the day Man fell
(Who, tasting Mercy, swallowed Hell).
And then I saw Death lovingly
take his long fingers from the scythe
to gather ants & worms & me
from out the muck wherein we writhed.
He laid me where my coffin sits
and nailed the lid with cigarettes.
He wove a lily garland sweet
which insects crawled upon to eat.
Then he laid my coffin down
in the lonesome graveyard ground.
Down he laid my coffin, by
the bed wherein my savior died.

From 'A Little Geste'

In the Beginning

On the jetty, our fingers shading
incandescent sky and sea,

my daughter stands with me.
'Boat! Boat!' she cries, her voice

in the current of speech cascading
with recognition's joys.

'Boat!' she cries; in spindrift
bobbling sails diminish,

but Kate's a joyous spendthrift
of her language's resources.

Her ecstasy's contagion
touches the whirling gulls

and turns their gibbering calls
to 'Boat! Boat!' Her passion

to name the nameless pulls her
from the syllabic sea.

She points beyond the jetty
where the uncontested sun

wimples the wakeless water
and cries, 'Boat!' though there is none.

But that makes no difference to Katy,
atingle with vision and word;

and why do I doubt that the harbor,
in the inner design of truth,

is speckled with tops'ls and spinnakers,
creased with the hulls of sloops?

Kate's word names the vision
that's hers; I try to share.

That verbal imagination
I've envied, and long wished for:

the world without description
is vast and wild as death;

the word the tongue has spoken
creates the world and truth.

Child, magician, poet
by incantation rule;

their frenzy's spell unbroken
defines the topgallant soul.

Exploration

I am who the trail took,
nose of whom I followed,
woodwit I confided in
through thorned-and-briared hallows;
favoring my right side for
clouds the sun had hemmed in.
Behind the North I sought daystar,
bore down highroads hidden
to undiscerning gaze.
My right, my right I turned to
on trails strangely unblazoned
where fistfive forkings burgeoned,
I took my right. Was destined,
among deerdroppings on the ridge
or chipmunk stones astrain
or hoofmucks in the swampcabbage
to err? Landmarking birch
selfmultiplied in malice till
woods reared a whitebarred cage
around my spinning eye. The spool
of memory had run out my yarn
and lost the last hank. Found
I the maze I wander in
where my right, trusted hand,
leads round and round a certain copse,
a sudden mound of stone,
an anthill humming in the rocks
an expectant tune?
Lacklearning now my knowledge is
of how to coax recalcitrant
ignition from cold engines,
or mate a fugue in either hand
on spinet or converse
in any tongue but stonecrop signs.
Clouds hump like battling bulls. The firs

lash me with angry tines,
shred my clothes. A windwhipped will
uncompassed, lacking fur or fang,
strange to these parts, yet whom the anthill
anticipating, sang.

Safari

You need an empty burlap
bag; rubber boots;
a forked longhandled stick.
You need nerves like roots

of the willow half underwater
that stiffen the trunk they grip
though that trunk holds boughs aquiver
at the quietest breath.

You kneel on the willow's knees
probing the fern-rimmed ditch
till an arrow furrows the water,
till quiet is cleft by hiss

and quick and true the sinew
tightens in your arm, in your throat
and true and quick the long stick
lunges: a thunderbolt

pinions the diamond head
where the forking tongue is set
immobilizing nothing
else of that undulant jet –

I see those brave safaris
and my triumphal returns,
the writhing bag that dangles
from the forked stick's horns,

that dangles over the rosebuds
staked to the trellis I passed,
home through the tended garden
my prize held fast

– 'To do *what* with those creatures?
You'll drown them in the drain at once!' – and dream
of a boy, rigid, goggling
down the manhole's gloom

at serpents hugely striding
in the diamonded darkness agleam
and thrashing the still black waters
till they foam and rise like cream.

Flushing Meadows, 1939

Lightning! Lightning! Lightning! Without thunder!
A zaggedy white trombone of lightshot, crackling
Between metallic globules, egglike, hugely
Aching in the corners of our eyes, –
The afterburn of electrocuted air
Sizzled into our ears and nostrils, half blinded
Us. We reeled into the dim sunshine
Groping a little, holding hands, still hearing
The confident vibrant voice of the sound system –
'Harnessed . . . power . . . unnumbered benefits . . .'
And this we pondered down the bedecked Concourse
Of Nations. A gold-robed King of Poland brandished
Crossed swords on horseback pedestaled on high;
The Soviet Citizen bore his sanguine star
Almost as high as that American flag
That snaffled in the smart wind perched atop
The Amusement Park's live parachute drop.
Trapped in antique mores, now the sun
Abandoned the International Pavilions
To miracles of manmade light. The trees
In their pots were underlit, revealing pasty
Backsides of their embarrassed leaves. We barked
The shins of our puppylove against the crowds
That swirled around us, swirled like fallen leaves
In the wind's vortex toward the Pool of Fountains:
Mauve and yellowing geysers surged and fell
As national anthems tolled, amity-wise,
From the State of Florida's Spanish Carillon.
What portent, in that luminous night to share
Undyingly, discovery of each other!
Helen, Helen, thy beauty is to me
Like those immutable emblems, huge and pure, –
One glimmering globe the world's will unifying
Beside spired hope that ravels the deep skies,
Our time's unnumbered benefits descrying
In their own light's shimmer, though the new dawn comes
With lightning, lightening in a murmur of summer thunder.

In the Days of Rin-Tin-Tin

In the days of Rin-Tin-Tin
There was no such thing as sin,
No boymade mischief worth God's wrath
And the good dog dogged the badman's path.

In the nights, the deliquescent horn of Bix
Gave presentiments of the pleasures of sex;
In the Ostrich Walk we walked by twos –
Ja-da, jing-jing, what could we lose?

The Elders mastered The Market, Mah-jongg,
Readily admitted the Victorians wrong,
While Caligari hobbled with his stick and his ghoul
And overtook the Little Fellow on his way to school.

Awoke into a Dream of Singing

Awoke into a dream of singing.
Birds amassed their gloried peals,
Drenching the deadwood with their ringing.
I could not breathe that air, all song.

Those trees, studded with autumn's plumage,
Bore no leaves that made no sound.
The fountain at their knees cascaded
Icicles. From brazen wound

The statue gushed. That air, so chill
With reedy-beaked insistent song,
Clotted fountain's-blood to crystal.
I could not breathe that air, all song.

From 'The City of Satisfactions'

A New Birth

While I turned in a warm cocoon
Man and Rome fell.
Furrows scarred the valleys.
Haggle, blow and toil
Echoed at the stony gates,
Yet discipleship to the seasons
Made gay the festival.

All that long labor made me
Who split my earthling skin
In a fallen wind, a dusty sky.
What patrimony I come by
Lies, an empty sack,
Shrivelled fables at my back.
This is a new birth I begin.

A Meeting

He had awaited me,
The jackal-headed.

He from Alexandria
In the days of the Dynasts,

I from Philadelphia
In a time of indecisions.

His nose sniffed, impassive,
Dust of the aeons.

A sneeze wrenched my brain
– I couldn't control it.

His hairy ears listen
Long. He is patient.

I sift tunes from the winds
That blast my quick head.

His agate eye gazes
Straight ahead, straight ahead.

Mine watch clocks and turn
In especial toward one face.

I thank Priestess of Rā
Who brought us together,

Stone-cutters of Pharaoh
And The Trustees of

The British Museum.
When with dog-eared Anubis

I must sail toward the sun
The glistering Phoenix

Will ride on our prow;
Behind the hound-voices

Of harrying geese
Sink the cities of striving,

The fiefdoms of change
With which we have done,

Grown in grandeur more strange,
More heroic than life was

Or the dark stream at peace,
Or wings singed in the sun.

The Chosen

I am the one that drew
The black cake from the fire.
Then the sun throbbed
With blood's accusations.

Skulking fox and ferret snarl
In the dry rocks
At my tread.
Trees lock their arms against me.

The buzzard whose hover
Over the living
Spreads dread
Stills the wind above me

Whatever the track I follow.
Stones speak:
I have no fellows.
What did I do among them,

When, till this day
My lusts were young
And I lived as they live,
Bruising the earth,

That was worse than their wrongs
Or deserving their worst
Who last night lived as I lived
And now fling me forth?

The Unchosen

I didn't feel good
Even when I
Drew a white one. My blood

Beat like the toll
Of a bell in a blizzard.
Still ashake with fear's dole,

I watched him stand
Right beside me, and smile,
The black cake in his hand.

Then my belfry of bone
Nearly cracked out of pity
And – it missed me by *one* –

Joy. A stark stroke
Silenced the sun.
We stood still, stunned.

Then he cried out and broke
From our ring,
Ran alone, ran alone,

Raced up the heath.
As the sun oozed and bled
His lengthening

Shadow made dread
Hackle our marrow.
He grew with our dread

Till he was a shadow,
The gobbet that looms
On nightmare heath,

Presentiment of death
Committing our dooms,
Guilty of life.

We breathed the one breath,
Then with the one
Lunge, the one yell

We picked up stones.
We flung stones at its head.
The sun boomed like a bell –

We returned together.
We roasted the meat together.
We drank, we rejoiced together.

We were safe. We felt good.

In That High House

In that high house half up a hill
A string linked your hand to my hand.
From the swollen sea that gnashed the shore
A road coiled round the hill's stone breast.
Our string pulls taut, frays, snaps apart.
The castle's ruined, a winter's tree.
You mustn't cry now, little son.
The rooftree's fallen and the moon
Through skeletal shadows lights the hall.
Beyond the broken door a road
Coils round the ridges of a hill
Where another house may stand
And your hand loop another hand
And when that filament frays and falls
In roofless walls remember us
When most together most alone.

The Pursued

Surely he'd outwitted them, outdistanced them and earned
Respite at this café. There goes the ferry.
Two trips risked in his own person, over
And back, and now, in this wig
Crossed again. Nobody knew him.
Coffee under the arbor, mission done,
Content. And then he recognized
The first signs –
Heat, hotter than the day's heat, swarming
And his skin parched, stretching
Tight about each finger; the eyes
Pounding: arbor, harbor,
Table, gable, all begin to swing
Up and forth, forth and up, up and so, until
Giddily earth grinds beneath him, shudders;
Sweat oozes icy on his neck now,
On shaking chest a shirt of seaweed crawls,
Iron table rat-tat-tat-tat-tats against his elbow
Though harbor's calm and arbor's still. You've seen
A stepped-on centipede left on the pavement,
Each limb's oracular gesticulations?
– Cutting through the scent of pear trees
Klaxons, baying, toil up up the highroad,
Vans of his other pursuers.

The City of Satisfactions

As I was travelling toward the city of satisfactions
On my employment, seeking the treasure of pleasure,
Laved in the superdome observation car by Muzak
Soothed by the cool conditioned and reconditioned air,
Sealed in from the smell of the heat and the spines
Of the sere mesquite and the seared windblast of the sand,
It was conjunction of a want of juicy fruit
And the train's slowdown and stopping at a depot
Not listed on the schedule, unnamed by platform sign,
That made me step down on the siding
With some change in hand. The newsstand, on inspection,
Proved a shed of greyed boards shading
A litter of stale rags.
Turning back, I blanched at the Silent Streak: a wink
Of the sun's reflection caught its rear-view window
Far down the desert track. I grabbed the crossbar
And the handcar clattered. Up and down
It pumped so fast I hardly could grab hold it,
His regal head held proud despite the bending
Knees, back-knees, back-knees, back-knees propelling.
His eyes bulged beadier than a desert toad's eyes.
His huge hands shrank upon the handlebar,
His mighty shoulders shrivelled and his skin grew
Wrinkled while I watched the while we reeled
Over the mesquite till the train grew larger
And pumping knees, back-knees, we stood still and
Down on us the train bore,
The furious tipping of the levers unabated
Wrenched my sweating eyes and aching armpits,
He leapt on long webbed feet into the drainage
Dryditch and the car swung longside on a siding
Slowing down beside the Pullman diner
Where the napkined waiter held a tray of glasses.
The gamehen steamed crisp-crust behind the glass.
I let go of the tricycle and pulled my askew necktie,
Pushed through the diner door, a disused streetcar,
A Danish half devoured by flies beneath specked glass,
Dirty cups on the counter,

A menu, torn, too coffeestained for choices, told
In a map of rings my cryptic eyes unspelled
Of something worth the digging for right near by
Here just out beyond the two-door shed.
The tracks were gone now but I found a shovel,
Made one, that is, from a rusting oildrum cover,
A scrap of baling wire, a broken crutch,
And down I heaved on the giving earth and rockshards
And a frog drygasped once from a distant gulley
And up I spewed the debris in a range
Of peaks I sank beneath and sweated under till
One lunge sounded the clunk of iron on brass
And furious scratch and pawing of the dryrock
Uncovered the graven chest and the pile of earth downslid
While under a lowering sky, sweatwet, I grasped and wrestled
The huge chest, lunged and jerked and fought it upward
Till it toppled sideways on the sand. I smashed it
Open, and it held a barred box. My nails broke
On the bars that wouldn't open. I smashed it
Open and it held a locked box. I ripped my knuckles
But couldn't wrest that lock off till I smashed it
Open and it held a small box worked
In delicate filigree of silver with
A cunning keyhole. But there was no key.
I pried it, ripped my fingers underneath it
But couldn't get it open till I smashed it
Open and it held a little casket
Sealed tight with twisted wires or vines of shining
Thread. I bit and tugged and twisted, cracked my teeth
But couldn't loose the knot. I smashed it
Open and the top came off, revealing
A tiny casket made of jade. It had
No top, no seam, no turnkey. Thimblesmall
It winked unmoving near the skinbreak
Where steakjuice pulsed and oozed. I thought aroma
Sifted, thinning till the dark horizon
Seemed, and then no longer seemed, a trifle
Sweetened. I knelt before

A piece of desert stone. When I have fitted
That stone into its casket, and replaced
The lid and set that casket in its box,
Fitted the broken top and set that box within
The box it came in and bent back the bars
And put it in the chest, the chest back in the hole,
The peaks around the pit-edge piled back in the pit,
Replaced the baling wire and crutch and oildrum cover
And pushed back through the diner, will the train
Sealed in from the smell of heat and mesquite
Envelop me in Muzak while it swooshes
Past bleak sidings such as I wait on
Nonstop toward the city of satisfactions roaring?
If I could only make this broken top
Fit snug back on this casket

'The Great Horse Strode Without a Rider'

The great horse strode without a rider.
He looked as though no bit had ever reined him,
No girthstrap squeezed the gloss of his firm belly.
The glass store windows mirrored him in broken
Images he smartly paced between.
His hooves precisely clapt upon the pavement.
Pistol-shots sound like his taut tattoo.
Pedestrians in ant-swarms elbowed doorways
Crouched beneath his image in the glass
On Commerce Avenue, until he came
To where it broadens under aisles of trees.
Now he was trotting and the trees dropped shadows
Flicking on and off his flanks in ripples.
His jaunty nostrils gathered all the wind in
That strained through sweetened lindens. Now he breathed
An easy laboring while criss-crossing feet
Rapped sharp *accelerandos*. In the houses
Watchers dropped their gaze from square glazed cages
To caress his rump. Then he was gone,
Past the furthest gatehouse by the roadside
Where roadsides run to thistles in the daisies,
And I though not astride him yet beside him
Moving with like movement to his speed
Now watch him break into a frolic canter.
His capers kick the clods up leaping after.
Now breasting upward toward the wind he gallops.
His mane whips like the backlash of sea-breakers
Over the ridge while I'm still struggling upward
Over the ridge. He's running down the headland.
He's far beyond me now and yet I see him
In clarity beyond the meed of sight.
His mighty movements pull me as the moon
Toward the vast intensity of heaven
Tugs the laggard tides. He's poised there, leaping
To for an instant hang as the hawk hangs, plunge then
Forefeet stretched to part the weedy froth
And disappear below the hill's rock brow.
Laboriously I clambered down the cliffside,

Pushed my way through wave-smashed bluffs past tide-pools,
Came at last to the broken stone declivity
Where spittled breakers, foam on rippled chests
And heads wind-tossed in their relentless oncome,
Lunged out of the sea to heave before me
The hugeness of their purpose, on, and on,
In charge on echoing charge against the shore.

From 'Striking the Stones'

The Way It Is

They were waiting here to say
This is the way it is

This is the way

I came bawling into their domain
Of harsher light
Remembering a place
Of purer light and messages
Passed across a darkened transom
From that place
Remembering

They said this is the way it is
In this light this dust
This scuffle for the scraps, bad blood
Between unequals   You'll get wise
You can break
Your heart against stones here
Remembering.

Counsellors, betake your
Covenants of convenience
To a place of stones,

I
Must lift the shadow of each shadow
To find the dooryard
To that place.

There

Who'd go out there

On the black, humped
Slithering snarl of the sea

Past splintered
Rock hulls

Of islands wrecked by wave

Unless drawn
Inward

By her nets of song?

Testament

A bare tree holds the fog in place.

It seeps out of irregularities
In gnarled twigs, those crevices
A nuthatch has picked clean

– One time there was a hill
Behind this tree
Dropped down,

A prospect of the tumbling
Breakers curled.

Fog has grown out of a tree.
I am the only
Thing moving

In this country.
No sky
Over no hill
Above no curved horizon,

The world contracts,

Interchange of codicils
Between one stem of taut limbs
In the damp halflight

Of this birdless day
And another.

In the Pitch of Night

White-throat beyond my window,
The sliver of your song
Pierces
The mist before the morning light
Shrivels the promises of night.

Your song
Changes nothing. The cold bay
Heaves and settles as before.
I cannot see you
In your cloudy tree.

Why do you thrust your silver knife
Into my silences? What undelivered
Letter will you open
Slitting the folded edges
Of my sleep?

It is darker
Before my open eyelids
Than in the clarity before
When I was hearing
From a burning tree

A sparrow sing.
I could all but see him in the blaze.
His unappeasable desire
Threaded across the sky
A testament of change,

Melting into song
Those pure resonances only
That echo
Without cease
Through discords dying all the day.

Instructions to a Medium, to be transmitted to the shade of W. B. Yeats, the latter having responded in a séance held on 13 June 1965, its hundredth birthday:

You were wrong about the way it happens,
You, unwinding your long hank of that old yarn
   Spun from our common dream since chaos first receded,
   As though a superannuated Druid were needed.

What looms now on that desert where the birds
Turn in their frenzy and scream uncomprehending?
   Not a cradled beast in whom divinity
   Could repossess the earth with fierce majesty;

We've seen the coming of a dispensation
Miniaturized in our set on the tabletop:
   Blazing from its pad, that rigid rocket
   No larger than the ballpoint pencil in my pocket

With its sophisticated systems for manoeuvre
And retrieval, the bloated astronauts within
   Plugged to cardiometers in weightless flight
   – Their radiant spirals crease our outer night.

No, you were wrong about the way it happens.
Our radar scorns all horoscopes. Where souls,
   Failing of perfection, fell toward birth,
   Junked satellites in orbit ring the earth

And circuitry has made the Tetragrammaton
As obsolescent as a daft diviner's rod.
   Yet you, a boy, knelt under Knocknarea
   Where the cragged mountain buffeted the sea

And knew a cave beside that desolate shore
Had been the gate through which Christ harrowed Hell.
   But what could knowledge of that sort be worth?
   Imagination would not rest; from that day forth

God-driven, you toiled through our long-darkening age
To do the work the gods require. In love, in rage,
   You wrote no verse but glorifies the soul.
   What's history, that we should be imprisoned

By some contention of the passing minute,
No sooner won than lost by those who win it?
   All action's but a strut between the wings.
   Our part you knew we each must play by heart,

By heart-mysteries that no invention changes
Though knowledge further than our wisdom ranges.
   'What matter though numb nightmare ride on top?'
   You knew there'd be a perturbation in the skies,

You knew, whatever fearful turn would come
By our contrivance, or immortal from the womb,
   Violence must break old tables of the law
   And old solemnities toward desecration draw,

But how conceive coherence with our power?
Old ghost, you seem to beckon from your tower –
   Moon-magic is the grammar of your speech,
   A cast of thought to keep within our reach

The tragic gaiety of the hero's heart
That blazes where the soul consumes in art
   All reality as faggots for its fire,
   Revealing the desired in the desire.

Then man, though prisoned in his mortal day,
In imagination dominates all time,
   Creates that past and future between which his way
   Unwinds with the fated freedom of a rhyme.

Words for Dr Williams

Wouldst thou grace this land with song?
  Well, go yodel your head off.
But if it's poems you want, then take a town
  with mills and chimneys, oil
Slithering on the river toward the falls,
  grit in the air, a man
Just off the night shift turning, tired yet strong
  to watch the girl who hurries
Toward a timeclock step down from the bus –
  slim ankles, one,
Two, and click click click swings past. The sun
  glints on her raincoat. There's
Your muse and hero. Stick around this town
  where people speak American
And love is possible – Your stethoscope
  held to our arteries
In sickness and in health you found some places
  where our own poems grow.

On the Industrial Highway

Approaching the Walt
Whitman Bridge you pass
an affluent world –

a subculture of spouts,
nozzles, ducts, a host
of snakes and ladders

in nests and thickets
or by tribes, laying
dinosaur farts

against the sun.
I drive slowly through the
stink and gawk at

shapes that no
familiarity breeds,
a ghostless city

called 'gas works,' never
meant for death or living.
A pipe pulses

flame in secret
code on the gashed sky.
Here are things

whose archetypes
have not yet been dreamed.
There's no more perfect

duct than these
ducts, pipes, facts
burdened with nothing

anticipating
unhappened memories,
visionary things.

Crop-Dusting

The mice rot in their tunnels in a field
Where phantom harvesters cut phantom grain.
A poisoned acre grows a poisoned yield.

Here skinny children stretch their hands in vain.
Their swollen bellies hurt, and are not healed.
A phantom blade has harvested their grain.

Night after night I see this land annealed
By draughts of fire and death that fall like rain.
One poisoned acre poisons all the field.

These are my crops. We harrow my domain.
The one who pays counts all for which he's billed.
A phantom harvester stacks phantom grain.

To own such wealth as this my heart I've steeled
And all but stilled the tumult in my brain.
My poisoned acre grows a poisoned yield.

Unable to be dispossessed by Cain,
In his accounts my civil tithes are sealed.
And how renounce the poisoning of this field,
Or be forgiven the reaping of its grain?

Shaking the President's Hand

Who'd be likely to forget
His brief squeeze by those brisk fingers,
The First Citizen's! The touch of kings
Was blessed, a gift to remedy
The King's Evil. Here
Where every man's a king,
What did I touch a President to cure?

Moving among the Creatures

Moving among the creatures
As the new light
Surges down this cliff, these trees, this meadow,
Brightening the shade among the alders
And shrivelling the dew on leaves,
They are contented in their bodies – I can tell it –
The squalling gulls delighted to be turning
Widdershins, their shadows swooping
Over rocks where startled deer
Clatter, flashing spindly shanks
And delicate hooves while underfoot
Even the uglies in their sticky skins
Exult, the woodfrogs clunking all the bells
In sunken steeples, till at my
Thick tread
They leap and scissor-kick away
While the withering leech,
Shrinking, enlarging, waving
Knobbed horns
Makes the stem shine
With silver spittle where he's gone.
I trip on vines, stumble in potholes
And long for something of myself that's in them,
In the gulls' windy coursing, in the frogs'
Brief cadenza, even in the slug's
Gift to leave
A gleaming track, spun
From his own
Slippery gut.

At Evening

At evening comes a certain hour
When the teeming world remembers
It is a hostage of the dead.

Then bend in homage
The tall trees whose sprinkle of seeds
Tickled the wind. The wind is dying.

This is the hour when dust
Gleams as the tired corona leans
Its bloodied head against the rim of sky

And the dark night girds
Beyond the pulsing stars
To drop its pomps of mourning down.

From windows of the houses come
Colloquial sounds and pungent odors,
Alien rhythms thrust against the night.

'He was the first who had returned'

He was the first who had returned
From that country
Of another tongue.

Speech, there,
Used purer forms of ecstasy than love
Here. Our actions fumble
With a gross vocabulary.

He makes the world
Around him glow
In simplicity of light.
His nouns are proverbs but their wisdom lies

Useless
In our boroughs of necessity,
Pure homage
Only known
When blood has crumpled, all its glories gone.

The Way He Went

He didn't go away
To the roll of drums
Or to annunciatory thunder
Of mantic voices,

He didn't leave by the long light
Of line-storms slashing doomed horizons
Or the guiding blink and dousing
Of little harbor lights,

He went by darkness and by daylight going
A silent way
Vacating endless
Acreages of parking-lots and marshes

Still
Then evening all atwitch with raucous birds
Ignorant of the emptiness that fell
Lighter than dew.

He went
And the stars shone hard and rocks
Arose in their accustomed risings
From the sea while broken clouds

Scudded around and closed against
Ragged towers of a city
Gathering tumults of electric signboards
Glowing in the sky where many colors

Made one color
As before.

The Victor

When the fight was over
And the enemy lay dead
The victor shuddered in a daze,
Holding the butchered head

Of one whose strength had all but matched his strength,
Whose wile he undid by his guile.
Proven, his own superiority.
Still he quakes, tasting in victory

Blood hated, yet prized.
He had put on
That murderous character, in foe despised,
And how suck air in innocence again?

Lines for Jack Clemo

author of *The Map of Clay*,
now blind and deaf,
a 'Prisoner of God'

I stand on gritty Goonamarris,
The four elements assail me.
How can my senses hold all Nature's
Clarity and the soil of man?

He, leonine before the firescreen, paces
The kingdom of deprivation's borders
Striking the stones to make them sing.
No land's so bleak he cannot find those stones:

His Adversary guards the glazed ground.
They wrestle head to head and wound to wound,
Then inward darkness burns away,
Shards of silence frame the essential psalm.

Another Country

Coming to a cavern in a valley,
Who would not explore?
His pineknot lit, he thrust a way
Past droppings on the mossy floor,
Past walls that gleamed and streamed with waters
Into a chamber none had known before
Save who drew in colors deep as blood
The great creatures on that sacred dome
– Horned Huntsman, and the Woman, Moon –
It was then he found the doorway
To another country. Darkness
There is brighter than familiar noon.
The light that lights that land's like lightning.
Its sudden crackle rends the skies.
                                    He tries
To tell a prospect of that country,
His words as much like lightning as the mutter
Of seared cloud
When the bolt's dazzle has come, and gone.

'It cannot come because desired'

It cannot come because desired,
It makes
Its own weather, its own time
Glowing
Like the phosphorescent wake
Of ships,
Mysterious tumult
Slitting the sensuous sea.

Love does not know
How we retrace
Together our most desperate seeking
Our most sacred place;

It's with these
Banal bodies
That we must
Make do,
Their strangely bulged and cherished
Curvatures, their folds, their flanks,
Their impermanent
Ageing surfaces
Concealing

Messages that we
Discover, each
The other's own
Rosetta Stone –

Love, I never hear
The brusque unpurposed clamor of the street
Or breathe the damp
Dolor that floods our city from the vast
Cool vats of space
But hold, an amulet against mischance,
Remembrance of your touch,
Your hands, your urgent hips,
The imperishable light, your sleeping face.

A Marriage

'Remember that farmer down in Maine
Who said to us, "I've been
An abandoned island
Since she's gone"?

– That's the hurt of proud flesh
We've known,
The heart's self-borne contagion
When you or I have parted us

With those rending, furious
Irretrievable accusations.
Each gulp of air keeps the wound fresh.
Left to the individual freedom

Of broken ends
We can't make meet, I roar
Off, a space-bound satellite
With no earth to encircle, adrift

In that unfinished void
Where nothing numbs the red scar
Of a burnt-out asteroid.
And yet I turn, seeking some tremor

Of your light,
Your heat,
Wherever in that emptiness
You are.'

'Who was it came'

Who was it came
Over the mountains bearing
Gifts we did not ask?

– Not the sapience of the thrush
Or the ant's perdurance,
Something a body might use –

Who was it brought
Cerements and a wrinkled skin,
A sour digestion

Over the mountains, offering
Crotchets and a rheumy gaze
And wits gone wandering?

Just when we thought to repossess
The taut frenzies of Chicago jazz
And bridal ardor

Here he comes,
Inexorable gaffer in an old hat
Croaking our names.

From 'Broken Laws'

Aphrodite

How could she come to us inviolate
From that uncomplicated country
Of pure feeling? History

Alters all it touches,
And if her image now is such
That we cannot know

Which sacred objects her slim hands
Held, still, her glance,
Resting a moment on our eyes,

Stays, then quickens with clamorous beat
The bursting heart abandoned to desire . . .
If some goatherd with his rude

Mattock, or pillager's keen sword
Gash the cover of her mound
To seize her, as though mortal,

From memory's chamber underground,
The imperfections of her image
Are not her imperfections, the scarred

Seam, the limb sheared
By avid diggers or the gnaw
Of vandal centuries. Her face

Requites the tribute of our awe,
Her body's lithe, incomparable grace
Drives imagination wild

Should it please her to appear
As the one in whose embrace
The love that is engendered is beguiled.

A Fortune

'All that I see is framed
On this one card. A reaper,
Bent, his gleaming blade unswung
And the grain like hair in the wind
Rippling, bent
Motionless, for the wind that moves it
Does not move. The sun,
Yes, the sun burns
An eyehole in metallic blue,
Pours a tunnel of shade
Beneath a foreground tree. There
The thighs, breasts,
Shoulders, face of a girl gleam
As though by moonlight
And the tree bursts
Into flower, the pattern
Of the petals intricate
As birdsong and her white
Arms reaching, reaching out . . . The slant
Horizon hangs
Above you curtaining a throne-room
Where the Queen of Hearts
Holds in her fierce grip
A sceptre like a sword.
On this bloodblack card
The silence
Swells with her exultance,
Her exactions.'

Over the Rim

Of this day hovers
The just design
This day tried
But failed to find,
All its busy creatures

Spurting with desires,
Spieling the recipes
Of their self-justifications
By which the mind
Of the entire world

This day betrayed
The perfection of our common
Lot, our clearest thought
Into these fragments, these
Wounds, self-serving anthems

And ridiculous longings – among them
You and I were for a moment
Together welded in a semblance
Of what this broken
Day left unattained.

In the Græco-Roman Room

I have seen 21 beautiful and naked
Aphrodites, each one arching
her small right foot, her slender
arms clasping the shift of wind
against her breasts. One can desire
what may scarcely be believed in,

one can admire the dozen Hercules
and Herakleses, archaic heroes
of the unprotected private parts,
so strong the skins of their
flayed lions seem
to grow from their own shoulders

– these, the idols of an Age of Error.
Not to be said, though, of the bronze
mouse $1\frac{1}{4}$
inches high blowing
a trumpet, one small paw and elbow
stopping his own ears.

A Historian

The dead again
Burst from their levelled graves
They reassemble on the hill
Ready for disastrous victory
Where a great empire fell
On its foe and fell

Again in the hot wide
Landscape of his mind
The captains sit astride
Their festooned chomping horses send
Battalions into certain
Enfilade

O they can never
Change the outcome they have fought
This battle over
Never knowing
Why they are there
Still following

Tattered pennants ignorant
Of trade routes or the pride
Of prince or diplomat whose ruse
Charges them to ride
The bloodspecked foaming crest
Of this riptide

No more than he can know
The soldier's brute obedience to orders
The captain's fealty to the general's plan
The commanders wrapped in webbed illusion
That their strategy will follow
Their will

Nor know the iron taste of fear
In throats that do not seem a part
Of the same contraption as the legs
Wildly going their own way
Or the gut that retches at the smell of blood
Or the heart

Booming its dark cannonade
Until the heartbeat or the battle ends.
The tallying of losses starts again.
The sky thickens with buzzards' wings.
They settle, gorge, and circle, waiting for
The future

A Trip

Our tickets
won't be honored
on this line?

But we've paid
full fares –
Look, we've brought

our lunches, packed
in paper bags
– And who are these

who take our places
singing, in the long
steel cone?

At the countdown
we stand
numbed

as castaways
on Turtle
Rock who watch

their frigate's sails
shrink to specks,
then nothing

where the sea
becomes the infinite
unfeatured blue.

A Special Train

Banners! Bunting! The engine throbs
In waves of heat, a stifling glare
Tinges the observation-car

And there, leaning over the railing,
What am I
Doing in the Orient?

Blackflies, shrapnel-thick, make bullocks
Twitch. The peasants stand
Still as shrines,

And look, in this paddy
A little boy is putting in the shoots.
He's naked in the sunlight. It's my son!

There he is again, in that
Field where the earth-walls meet.
It's his play-time. See, his hands are smeared

With mud, and now his white
Back is flecked with ash, is seared
By embers dropping from the sky –

The train chuffs past. I cry
Stop! Stop! We cross another paddy,
He's there, he's fallen in the mud, he moans my name.

A Waking

The fact that the sun has once again with sharp claws
Pried
Open the eye of the day
Does not establish
The necessity
Or recurrence
Of any of the terms

Like light or day and
Night we awaken
Knowing
That where we've been has led us only
To the edge
Of this field

And at our backs
Memories
Stolid as boulders cracked
By long-forgotten frozen rains
Do not advance
Toward the grackles
Whose strident plaint proclaims
Dominion
Of the dew

A Marked Man

He has this wound
Like an open mouth
He keeps it hidden
A hand cupped on a scream

But it's there just the same
When he's in the bleachers
Or sits at the bar
Like a lipless mouth it's

Moaning his name

A distinguishing mark
For each gaze in the ballroom
All eyes in the ballpark
Why would they look somewhere else?

It doesn't seem likely
To close up in a pale stitch
And knit itself cured
Without a word

For whenever it's almost
About to grow sound
He's liable to poke a finger
Back in the wound

Which moans thereupon
An open mouth
He has this mark
I could tell you about

Resolution

A single egg hatched every shape that swarms.
The hand that ordained Chaos made the Forms.

A Dreamer

Awakened by the clarity of dream
As the train pitched forward in a rush careening
Down the mountain – Who wouldn't scream
When brakes fail and the conductor
Leaps from hurtling car? It was good,
Good to clutch the reasonableness of terror,
There was reassurance in that real
Fall, real crags, a landscape of sensible
Disaster, not this nameless, numb
Dread, the humming sun a poisoned stinger.

A Casualty

Ever since he's arrived in this country
Certain cells
Are dying, and the body's

Tolerance for liquids, foods
Declines, for medicaments, for air.
No tolerance for pleasure

As the exfoliations of the nerve-ends
By a lifetime's effort disciplined
To fine discriminations of desire

Twitch – now their ghosts
Throb in fire
Beyond the charred stumps of feelings.

Nobody's love can reach
Into the purity
Of such isolation.

In the instant of his pain's surcease
He recalls as in a rearview mirror
A pheasant glimpsed beside the road

His fender struck last summer
Half its feathers
Scattered like a fallen cloud

In convulsive trials to rise
Wildly unable just to acquiesce to
What glazed the golden pupils of its eyes.

Summer Solstice

Who's to tell the night heron
This night merits his observation
Or inform the carpenter bee
Of the day's singularity?

Only the membrane in the tissue
Of the algae or the eye
Steeped in ancestral memory
Retentive of stimuli

Has that calendrical
Instinct by which in France
On this day children strew the road with petals
Men burn a paper goat the women dance

Singing

This season
Belongs to the creatures
Peepers claim the nights

Sparrow thrush and skreaking waxwing
Extrapolate toward morning
Their cadenzas of a gilded day

Instinctual calls whose importunity
Pleases, as though the webbed
Desirous song and aubade of the swamp sparrow

Were notes that we remembered singing
Once, and yearn after
Recollecting how to sing

The Sounds

No use to make a tape
Recording of the liftoff
Or incorporate the sounds

The oil rig emits
In our suite – not
These the true ground

The ordained cadences
For rendering the thought
Which music is

Suggested by vestigial
Bird's whistle now or wailed
Snatch on boy's harmonica

This Silence

In this silence
Hear the breathing
Mouths that suckle

At the breast
Of night –
Is it the wind now

Or the glint of their
Exhalations tousling
Trees across

Whose faces brim
The milky
Rivulets

Aubade

Weaned from moon
By whitening sky

The still cove
Swells as the tide fills

There is no quenching water's
Thirst for light

I am the Sun

I am the sun the sun says
All that's scorched beneath my eye
Is mine   We were just going the winds sigh
What will become of us the leaves cry

Nowhere to go mutters the maple
Grizzled in its skin of wrinkles
What will become of us the lovers
Do not think to wonder in the dappled

Sun thrust through the wind-tossed leaves
Where head on breast and thigh at rest on thigh
Find such delight they'd take the world for love's
Body that cannot change or die

Snatches for Charles Ives

All those long dead New England farm boys
Sprang unarmed from R. W. Emerson's brain.
Where they fell they since have lain,
We forgot them like an old song out of mind,

Forgot their succor by the roadside spring,
Their probities before an angry God.
That upright Judge they judged them by is gone.
And who recalls the beehive hymnal drone

Uplifted souls made as they made concord?
What joy they found who found joy in the Word!
What martial airs were theirs, the fifetune boy's
Calliope that piped them, gay in blue

Files toward those backgrounds of ripped trees
And shattered waggons we've seen in Brady's
Photographs . . . They lie there where they've fallen,
All tent fires out, all camaraderies forgotten.

Torchlight parades! Magnetic energy of crowds!
Temperance and Tippecanoe! All those causes
Lost for long, dwindling with memory's losses,
Restored by these wild chords and sweet discords.

From 'The Center of Attention'

The Poem

Arriving at last,

It has stumbled across the harsh
Stones, the black marshes.

True to itself, by what craft
And strength it has, it has come
As a sole survivor returns

From the steep pass.
Carved on memory's staff
The legend is nearly decipherable.
It has lived up to its vows

If it endures
The journey through the dark places
To bear witness,
Casting its message
In a sort of singing.

After God

'The Jews have a Fancy, that when our Almighty
Creator befpangled the Heavens with the *Stars of
Night,* He left a Space near the Northern Pole,
unfinifhed and unfurnifhed, that if any *After-God*
fhould lay claim to Deity, a challenge to fill up
that fpace might Eternally confute it.'
                                    —Cotton Mather

Who keeps his ceaselessly attentive eye
Upon the flight and fall
Of each Polaris through the wide feast-hall
Of the sky,
So like the life of man from dark
To dark in a little space,

Who in this bowling alley spins
Balls of light
At the back of the North Wind
Careening as their plastic skins
Mirror widdershins
Our sponsored images,

Who flings bright strands of platinum hair
And unpointed needles wandering
Through the frozen stratosphere
In a confusion
Of jagged rays
Until True North is lost,

Who deafens Aurora Borealis
With climbing fire,
Who spurts with the desire
That blazes and subsides in ashen
Droppings of contagion
After the whirlwind,

Him we beseech
As adepts who would scan and preach
The Providences of His will.
Be done, send us a sign
That we may read
By the shrivelled light of our gelded sun

The sentence of our sufferings.
His blood flames now
Against the Northern sky.
He walks among us, visible.
The next dawn brings
A vacant hour that sacrifice can fill.

An Old Photo in an Old Life

A squad of soldiers lies beside a river.
They're in China – see the brimmed gables piled
On the pagoda. The rows of trees are lopped
And the Chinese soldiers have been stopped
In their tracks. Their bodies lie
In bodily postures of the dead,

Arms bound, legs akimbo and askew,
But look how independently their heads
Lie thereabouts, some upright, some of the heads
Tipped on their sides, or standing on their heads.
Mostly, the eyes are open
And their mouths twisted in a sort of smile.

Some seem to be saying or just to have said
Some message in Chinese just as the blade
Nicked the sunlight and the head dropped
Like a sliced cantaloupe to the ground, the cropped
Body twisting from the execution block.
And see, there kneels the executioner

Wiping his scimitar upon a torso's ripped
Sash. At ease, the victors smoke. A gash
Of throats darkens the riverbed. 1900. The Boxer
Rebellion. Everyone there is dead now.
What was it those unbodied mouths were saying?
A million arteries stain the Yellow River.

The Center of Attention

As grit swirls in the wind the word spreads.
On pavements approaching the bridge a crowd
Springs up like mushrooms.
They are hushed at first, intently

Looking. At the top of the pylon
The target of their gaze leans toward them.
The sky sobs
With the sirens of disaster crews

Careening toward the crowd with nets,
Ladders, resuscitation gear, their First
Aid attendants antiseptic in white duck.
The police, strapped into their holsters,

Exert themselves in crowd-control. They can't
Control the situation.
Atop the pylon there's a man who threatens
Violence. He shouts, *I'm gonna jump* –

And from the river of upturned faces
– Construction workers pausing in their construction work,
Shoppers diverted from their shopping,
The idlers relishing this diversion

In the vacuity of their day – arises
A chorus of cries – *Jump!*
Jump! and *No* –
Come down! Come down! Maybe, if he can hear them,

They seem to be saying *Jump down!* The truth is,
The crowd cannot make up its mind.
This is a tough decision. The man beside me
Reaches into his lunchbox and lets him have it.

Jump! before he bites his sandwich,
While next to him a young blonde clutches
Her handbag to her breasts and moans
Don't   Don't   Don't   so very softly

86

You'd think she was afraid of being heard.
The will of the people is divided.
Up there he hasn't made his mind up either.
He has climbed and climbed on spikes imbedded in
    the pylon

To get where he has arrived at.
Is he sure now that this is where he was going?
He looks down one way into the river.
He looks down the other way into the people.

He seems to be looking for something
Or for somebody in particular.
Is there anyone here who is that person
Or can give him what it is that he needs?

From the back of a firetruck a ladder teeters.
Inching along, up up up up up, a policeman
Holds on with one hand, sliding it on ahead of him.
In the other, outstretched, a pack of cigarettes.

Soon the man will decide between
The creature comfort of one more smoke
And surcease from being a creature.
Meanwhile the crowd calls *Jump!* and calls *Come down!*

Now, his cassock billowing in the bulges of Death's
    black flag,
A priest creeps up the ladder too
What will the priest and the policeman together
Persuade the man to do?

He has turned his back to them.
He has turned away from everyone.
His solitariness is nearly complete.
He is alone with his decision.

No one on the ground or halfway into the sky can know
The hugeness of the emptiness that surrounds him.
All of his senses are orphans.
His ribs are cold andirons.

Does he regret his rejection of furtive pills,
Of closet noose or engine idling in closed garage?
A body will plummet through shrieking air,
The audience dumb with horror, the spattered street . . .

The world he has left is as small as toys at his feet.
Where he stands, though nearer the sun, the wind is chill.
He clutches his arms – a caress, or is he trying
Merely to warm himself with his arms?

The people below, their necks are beginning to ache.
They are getting impatient for this diversion
To come to some conclusion. The priest
Inches further narrowly up the ladder.

The center of everybody's attention
For some reason has lit up a butt. He sits down.
He looks down on the people gathered, and sprinkles
Some of his ashes upon them.

Before he is halfway down
The crowd is half-dispersed.
It was his aloneness that clutched them together.
They were spellbound by his despair

And now each rung brings him nearer,
Nearer to their condition
Which is not sufficiently interesting
To detain them from business or idleness either,

Or is too close to a despair
They do not dare
Exhibit before a crowd
Or admit to themselves they share.

Now the police are taking notes
On clipboards, filling the forms.
He looks round as though searching for what he came
    down for.
Traffic flows over the bridge.

The Translators' Party

The great Polish
Emigré towered
Over the American
Poets at the party
For the contributors
Who'd wrested and wrought
The intractable consonants
Of Mickiewicz
Into a sort
Of approximate English,

Till Auden went over
To Jan Lechon,
Half a foot taller
Than the rest of us scribblers
And would-be reviewers,
Those venerables
For an hour reliving
A continent's culture,
Aperçus in the lilting
Accents heard

In cafés in Warsaw,
Vienna, Kracow . . .
One with the fiction
Of civilized discourse
In his native diction
Still entertainable
In imagination,
The other among
Aliens, aliens
In an alien tongue

For whom the greatness
Of the poet Adam
Mickiewicz can only
Be indirectly
Expounded, like Chopin's
Shown in slide-lectures
To a hall of wearers
Of battery-powered
Audiophones,
For whom his own poems

Cannot be known but
In deaf-and-dumb hand-signs,
No shades of his sounds, his passionate
Rhythms twisted.
His poems are stateless.
Yet it's Lechon's laughter
That I remember,
With one who could summon
A world lost in common
For an hour's reversal

Of an age's disaster
– Never known
To us in our *Times*
A fortnight after
Who read he was found
'Apparently fallen'
From his high window,
That voice
Stilled now
On New York's alien ground.

The Princess Casamassima

After digging in the rubble of the ruined house
For nine days
They've found a *third* corpse –
No fingerprints; no hands.
One leg and the head blown off.
The story in the *Times*
Didn't even tell
The sex of the torso . . .

These were some of the people
Who'd take power to the people
In their own hands.
All their questions have one answer.
Dynamite.
Makes non-negotiable demands
For an apocalypse,
In case of survivors.

Once, another world ago,
There was a girl I never dreamed
Would be like them:
She seemed to lack nothing
– Looks, friends, certainly a silver
Spoon had stirred her porringer –
She'd sit scribbling
Notes in the next to the back row,

But I can't remember now
One word she wrote for me.
– Good God,
Was it something *I* said
About Thoreau
Shorted her fuse? Oh,
Such unbalanced, mad
Action is surely extra-curricular –

If the discourse of our liberal arts
Which entertains all rival truths as friends
And rival visions reconciles
Could but bring the pleasures of its wholeness
To a mind
Rent by frenzy –
But how conceive what hatred
Of the self, turned inside-out, reviles

The whole great beckoning world, or what desire
Sentenced the soul
To that dark cellar where all life became
So foul
With the pitch of rage,
Rage, rage, rage to set aflame
Father's house – what can assuage
That fire or that misfire?

Power

'My life is a one-billionth part
Of history. I wish I was dead.'

He rips the page from his notebook.
Litter in a rented room.

The neighbors will barely remember
His silence when they said Hello.

They'll not forget his odd smile.
Nobody comes to see him.

When he thinks of his folks he smiles oddly.
'It was broken but was it a home?'

At night, the wet dream. Arising,
He is afraid of women.

In his notebook, 'Power over people!'
His job, scouring pots in a hash-house.

At last he will pick up a girl.
She'll think, Does he ever need love –

But I don't like him at all.
Her Mom will hang up on his phone call.

One day he will fondle a snub-nosed
Pistol deep in his pants.

What is his aim? The TV,
Even bumper stickers remind him

Who has the face and the name
His name and smile will replace.

His trigger will make him bigger.
He will become his victim.

When he steps from his rented room
History is in his hands.

The Sonnet

(Remembering Louise Bogan)

The Sonnet, she told the crowd of bearded
        youths, their hands exploring
            rumpled girls,
            is a sacred

vessel: it takes a civilization
        to conceive its shape or know
            its uses. The kids
            stared as though

a Sphinx now spake the riddle of
        a blasted day. And few,
            she said, who would
            be *avant-garde*

consider that the term is drawn
        from tactics in the Prussian
            war, nor think
            when once they've breached

the fortress of a form, then send
        their shock troops yet again
            to breach the form,
            there's no form –

. . . they asked for her opinion of
        'the poetry of Rock.'
            After a drink
            with the professors

she said, This is a bad time,
        bad, for poetry.
            Then with maenad
            gaze upon

the imaged ghost of a comelier day:
        I've enjoyed this visit,
            your wife's sheets
            are Irish linen.

Tree

This is a slice of the oldest
Tree the world has known.

When this outside ring grew in the forest
Chainsaws and a tractor brought it down.

When the tree's husk was this narrow ring,
Washington's troops were shivering;

In this ring's year the Tartar horde
Drenched earth with blood of the conquered;

In this year, a black ring –
As a cross was a tree hung;

Gilgamesh journeyed toward the dark
When this ring swelled beneath the bark;

When sap rose here the tree was great
With blossom, with unfallen fruit;

Here, fed by roots that reached far down
To suck milk out of the earth,

These heartwood rings grew firm. Their girth
Braced high boughs, and a spreading crown

Held unchanging stars as leaves;
The tree propped up the heavens

And gods drowsed in its shade
Then, before time was made.

These dates of interest are each marked now
On the cracked disc by a cardboard arrow.

Dogfish

He lurks and sidles away out of sight. But when you stand
At the rail of a cruiser twenty miles from land
Hauling the inert haddock and sluggish cod

Suddenly one, then two, three, four of the lines pull
Taut in a tangle, go slack and taut again with a caught
Life fighting in jerks and rushes deep under the keel,

Then in a battle of shouts, bent rods, and whirring reels
And curses and the pulling of lines in a net of knots
Tied together by a wild shuttle, alive and enraged,

He's gaffed and over the rail, slashing our boots with his tail,
A streak of muscle and will, writhing and gnashing until
The mate hands me the hatchet to hack his head off

– I see that struggle in the mind's slow motion still:
Dogfish, smallest of sharks, who just was the terror
That rocketed through the somnambulant schools

Of weakfish fated for his belly or our chowder,
His head atilt, the underslung jaw of sawblades ripping
White flesh in the deep green dimness.

A stinking gobbet of squid on my hook was
His undoing. Wedged in his ravenous throat
The barbed iron, the invisible cord, relentless.

My arm is unable to stop. I beat the blade
Where the gills writhe with a life of their own and the head
Flops free. His body as long as my arm jerks to a dead stop.

Blood

At a wolf's wild dugs
When the world was young
With eager tongue
Twin brothers tugged,

From foster mother
Drew their nurture.
Her harsh milk ran
Thence in the blood of man,

In the blood of kings
Who contrived the State.
What wolvish lust to lead the pack
The memory of that taste brings back.

Rats

To rid your barn of rats
You need a watertight
Hogshead two-thirds full
You scatter your cornmeal
On the water
Scattered as though all
The barrel held was meal
And lean a plank against the rim
And then lay down –

This is *important*!

– A wooden chip the size
To keep one rat afloat
He'll rid your barn of rats
He'll leap into your meal
He'll sink he'll swim and then he'll
See the chip
He'll slither aboard and squeal
And another rat beneath your eaves
Will stop
        and listen,

And climb down to that barrel
And walk that plank and smell
The meal and see meal
And one rat
He'll hear that rat squeal
I'll get mine he'll think and he'll
Leap in and sink and swim
He'll scramble on that chip

– Now watch him! –

He'll shove the first rat down
In the water till he'll drown
He'll rid your barn of rats
He'll shiver and he'll squeal
And a rat up on your rafter
Will hear,
        and stop,
                and start
Down the beam
Coming after
With one intent as in a dream –

He'll rid your barn of rats.

Eagles

When things are creatures and the creatures speak
We can lose, for a moment, the desolation
Of our being

Imperfect images of an indifferent god.
If we listen to our fellows then,
If we heed them,

The brotherhood that links the stars in one
Communion with the feathery dust of earth
And with the dead

Is ours. I have seen bald eagles flying,
Heard their cries. Defiant emblems of
An immature

Republic, when they spread their noble wings
They possess the earth that drifts beneath them.
I've learned how

Those savage hunters when they mate are wed
For life. In woods a barbarous man shot one
In the wing.

He fluttered to an island in the river.
After nearly half a year, someone,
Exploring, found

Him crippled in a circle of the bones
Of hen and hare his partner brought to him.
Close above,

She shrieked and plunged to defend her helpless mate.
Eagles, when they mate, mate in the air.
He'll never fly.

His festered wing's cut off, he's in the zoo.
They've set out meat to tranquillize his queen
And catch her too.

Who'll see them caged yet regal still, but thinks
Of eagles swooping, paired in the crystal air
On hurtling wings?

Shell

I would have left the me that was then
Clinging to a crack in the bark of the tree,

Stiffened in wind, the light translucent,
A brittle shell that had the shape of me;

And down the back a split through which had burst
A new creature, from mean appearance free,

Swaying now where the topmost boughs of the tree sway
At the center of the sound that's at the center of the day.

Burning Bush

If a bush were to speak with a tongue of fire
To me, it would be a briar;
The barberry, bearing unreachable droplets of blood,
Or, bristling in winter, rugosas with their red hoard

Of rosehips and a caucus of birds singing.
Come Spring, in a burst at the road's turn,
A snowblossom bank of the prickly hawthorn;
Or drooping in June on their spiny, forbidding stem

Blackberries ripe with the freight of dark juice in them.
If I should listen to a bush in flame
Announce the Unpronounceable Name
And demand requital by a doom

On my seed, compelling more
Than I'd answer for, what no one else would ask,
That voice of fire would blaze in a briar
I cannot grasp.

Window

Is it no more than an eyehole
On the outside scene
Making everything
– The snow, the runaway dog,
The boys brawling and the car
Skidding against the tree –
Content to be contained
Within a reasonable frame?
Or could it be

A casement dividing
A real observer from a view
Of untrammelled possibility,
Its pane connecting
A man in a room in
Steam heat and a battered chair
With his future
Which he could not see
Were it not there?

Perhaps it's the lens that allows
Errant swifts and swallows
In a downward swoop
Of their tumbling flight
To glimpse the man waiting
For the future to happen –
While he's caged in time
They're free to look in,
And its gift is insight.

Wherever

North

For reasons of their own the red-winged blackbirds
Have gathered in a cloud. They fall like snow.

The skies, the trees, the fields are black with blackbirds,
Black with the pandemonium of their cries.

The only place more desolate than this one
Is this, when the last straggling birds have flown.

East

Always the mysterious
Promise of a new day.

This is the place
Of birth, the distant home

Of the future
God. Until he come

There is no entrance
There. What awaits us we

Can know only
By our deliverance.

South

Here you hoard the green
Hieroglyphs of morning
All the baffled afternoon.

West

This is the home of the setting sun
Of the past
Of the long procession
Of the dead.

You can journey toward it forever
Without arriving.
Each of your footsteps enlarges behind you
The lost land you seek.

The Wanderer

This body that has fastened
Itself to the wanderer

Who hastens with mysterious
Balked purposes,

These hands that answer,
This face that turns

At the calling
Of the name

That I am wearing
Like one shoe

– How did I come
In all this gear

Among so few
Clues to where I've come from

Or where
I am to go?

Runner

There's not enough air in the sky for his lungs to gulp
A full draught that would quench the heat in his blood.
His heart is about to pound apart and his legs
Are flogged slaves from a conquered country.
They've trodden the ground till they're numb.

He has run all morning and run while the sun in the heavens
Lurched to the top of its climb and hung, unmoving
All that long noon, spreading the drone of its heat
And all that while his dogged feet
Ran on in the dust, and ran

Past gates that opened and doors that tilted ajar
On quiet rooms and gardens where fountains sighed
And languorous women as the light streamed from their hair
Looked up with secretive smiles that said
'At last you've arrived here,'

Yet still he plods on though behind him his shadow grows
    longer
And the shadows of trees are meshed with their boughs and
    their trunks.
That unending road he treads in a narrow passage
– By night will he know that the path he follows
Is the earth's wheel, spinning and spinning?

Sickness

He becomes the terrain an enemy force
Advanced on, spread out and dug into,

Mounting artillery in his head.
Siege guns all night long.

Blinded by bloodshot, he can't get through
To his own HQ.

They've poisoned his well. His nerves
Have been sabotaged,

His body's a burned-out battlefield, burning.
There's little fight left in him.

He'd put out the white flag if he could
Discover to whom to surrender.

He'd clear out of here if he could
Only hold himself steady

– His back is shaking, his legs
Twitch like a stepped-on spider's.

He is drained, drained white,
White as a midnight frost

And then in a deep sleep it's all over.
Come morning, he's a new man.

Evening

As a corpse
Bleeds
In the presence of its murderers

The scars
Of this grey sky
Burst again,

The wounds
Gush. On our hands,
The stain.

A Dread

It can be practically nothing, the nearly invisible
Whisper of a thought unsaid.
Pulsing, pulsing

At the bland center of a blameless day
It spreads its filaments through the world's
Firm tissues,

Relentless as an infection in the blood
Of one's own child, or a guilt
Time won't assuage.

Thought I Was Dying

Like a bucket
With a hole

I couldn't find
Just felt the seeping

Of my life
As it was leaving

My wife my children
Drifting away

My head empty
My hands my heart

Drained and void
The bed cold

I thought it's hard
To leave my life

With each breath
A little less

In the veins whistling
Till the sun shone black

As though I never
Could come back

Vows

I meet him in the spaces
Between the half-familiar places
Where I have been,
It's when I'm struggling toward the door
Of the flooded cellar
Up to my crotch in a cold soup
Of my father's ruined account books
There, like an oyster cracker
Floats my mother's Spode tureen
(The one they sold at auction
When the market was down) –

Then just outside
Before I'm in the trooptrain on the siding
Spending the vivid years
Of adolescence and the war
With dented messkit in hand
Always at the end
Of a frozen chowline
Of unappeased hungers,
He appears –

Listen, kid,
Why do you bug me with your reproachful
Silent gaze –
What have I ever
Done to you but betray you?
To which he says
Nothing.

Listen, I'd forget if I could
Those plans you made
For stanching the blood
Of the soul that spread
Its cry for peace across the unjust sky,
I wouldn't give it a thought if I

Could only not
Remember your vows
To plunge into the heat
Of the heart and fuse
With the passionate Word
All thought,
All art –

Come, let's go together
Into the burning
House with its gaping door.
The windows are all alight
With the color of my deeds,
My omissions.
It's our life that's burning.
Is it ever too late to thrust
Ourselves into the ruins,
Into the tempering flame?